Guiding

Successful

Six Sigma

Projects

an oriel incorporated publication

Table of Contents

Introduction

Increasingly, anyone in an organization may be called on to see that an improvement effort is completed on time and achieves results that are worth the investment.

But how can you tell if an improvement or design effort is going well? How can you tell if the right work is being done?

That's where **Guiding Successful Six Sigma Projects** comes in.

This handy guide can help anyone who takes part in, or oversees, an improvement or design effort. It summarizes roles, project steps, and key points you need to check throughout a project. Whether you are a manager, project sponsor, Master Black Belt, or Black Belt, you can use this guide to:

- Plan agendas for periodic review meetings with a team
- Review the critical checkpoints and questions before or during a meeting with a project team
- Create a checklist or chart to monitor progress of a project
- Determine which projects or efforts are being done well and deserve recognition
- Determine what level of effort and resources may be needed in a project

Project participants or team members can also use this guide to understand what their managers will expect of them at various stages in a project.

Six Sigma

Six sigma is a method for measuring how well a process is performing relative to customer requirements. A process with little variation will be better able to meet customer requirements than one that has a lot of variation. To improve process sigma, an organization generally needs to reduce the variation in existing products, processes, or services. New products, processes, and services are designed to consistently meet customer requirements from the start.

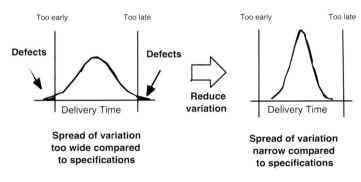

Spread of variation too wide compared to specifications

Reduce variation

Spread of variation narrow compared to specifications

This guide will help you focus on the factors that are central to six sigma: customers, data, and process. For each step, it highlights what is important to the customers, what process changes are needed to meet the customers' requirements, and what data supports this.

Project Selection

Selecting appropriate projects is critical for the success of both improvement and design efforts.

To be successful, a company's project selection methodology must:

- Link improvement/design efforts to strategic priorities
- Have involvement at all levels of the company
- Be able to measure the effect of improvement/design efforts

The following criteria are useful in selecting design and improvement projects:

The process or project is related to a key business issue	
We have or can get customer input on this issue	
Management does or would give this project high priority	
I can easily identify starting and ending points for the process	
Collecting data on the current process is relatively easy (may not be necessary for Design)	
There is an appropriate probability of success	
The process completes one cycle at least every day or so (may not be necessary for Design)	
I can identify what a "defect" is for this process	
The problem/gap I need to investigate or improve is stated as a target or need, not a solution	
I know who the process owner is	
The sponsor of this project has the ability to commit time and resources	
The process will not be changed by another initiative any time in the near future	

What's in This Guide?

This guide addresses the management of both improvement and design projects.

Managing Improvement Projects:

This guide divides the improvement process into steps. The steps used here are based on the Joiner 7 Step Method™ for problem solving and improvement and the DMAIC method of process improvement. These methods are closely related and share a common set of outcomes and goals, so we have combined them into the model shown below.

DMAIC	Joiner 7 Step Method™	This Guide
DEFINE	Project	**D**EFINE: Project
MEASURE	Current Situation	**M**EASURE: Current Situation
ANALYZE	Cause Analysis	**A**NALYZE: Causes
IMPROVE	Solutions	**I**MPROVE: Solutions
	Results	**I**MPROVE: Results
CONTROL	Standardization	**C**ONTROL: Standardization
	Future Plans	**C**ONTROL: Future Plans

Most standard improvement approaches use similar steps. So this guide will be useful to organizations that use other approaches as well.

Managing Design Projects:

The steps used in the design methodology are based on Oriel's Design for Excellence methodology (DESGN). This method is similar to the DMADV method. Both share common overall outcomes and goals, although the activities in the third and fourth steps are organized a bit differently. The table below shows how the two methods are related.

DMADV	DESGN
Define	**D**efine Project
Measure	**E**stablish Requirements
Analyze	**S**elect Concept
Design	**G**enerate Design
Verify	Impleme**N**t Design

For Both Improvement and Design:

The description of each step includes:

- **Goal:** The reason for doing the work in this step
- **Output:** What you should look for as a product of this work
- **Critical Checkpoints:** The milestones the team should reach in this step and for which you should get evidence
- **Relevant Tools:** A list of data collection, data analysis, and planning tools that the team can use to do the work in this step
- **Useful Questions:** Questions you can ask the person or team working on the project

In the back of the guide, you'll find an appendix including a glossary, information on roles and toll-gate reviews, review templates, and process sigma computation flowcharts and worksheets. The worksheets will show you how to convert a familiar measure such as process yield to process sigma.

Improvement Project Review

DEFINE: Project

Goal:

Define the project's purpose and scope

Output:

A clear statement of the intended improvement and how it will be measured

Critical Checkpoints:

- Problem or gap defined and documented
- Key internal measures or performance indicators chosen and defined, and goals for improvement set
- Customer needs identified for appropriate customer segments
- High-level process map developed

Relevant Tools:

Flowcharts, Pareto charts, time plots, control charts, Gantt charts, project plans, charter, communication plans, and other change management tools

Useful Questions:

- What problem or gap are you addressing?
- Why is this project important?
- What are the key measures or performance indicators?
    - How are the measures or performance indicators defined?
    - How will you know if things improve?
    - What is the current performance level?
- What are the major steps of the process you will be improving?
    - Who are the suppliers?
    - What are the inputs?
    - What are the outputs?
- What impact will closing the gap or solving the problem have on customers?
    - Who are the customers?
    - Are there relevant customer segments?
    - What data do you have to understand customer requirements?
- What measures are important to each customer segment? How do you know?
- What are the boundaries of this project?
- What are the business reasons for completing this project?
- Show me your project schedule. What project milestones have you established?

MEASURE: Current Situation

Goal:

Focus the improvement effort by gathering information on the current situation

Output:

A more focused problem statement and baseline process sigma

Critical Checkpoints:

- The problem or gap more localized
- Localization demonstrated with appropriate data analysis and tools
- Detailed process maps developed for critical parts of the relevant processes
- Key measures charted to establish baseline
- Process sigma calculated

Relevant Tools:

Data collection tools such as checksheets and concentration diagrams, flowcharts, Gage R&R, operational definitions, sampling, Pareto charts, time plots, control charts, frequency plots, stratification, and process sigma calculation

Useful Questions:

- What problem or gap are you addressing?
  - Where, when, and how often does the problem occur?
  - How severe is it?
- If appropriate, show me your flowchart or other sketch of the situation.
  - How did you create it? Validate it?
  - What did you learn from it? Is the process actually used?
- What data did you collect? How did you collect it?
  - What did you do to ensure that the data collection process was reliable and valid?
- What does the data tell you about the problem or gap?
- Show me the charts or graphs you used to analyze your data.
- What stratifying factors did you analyze?
- How did you define defect, unit, and opportunity?
- What is the current process sigma?
- Have you found any "quick hit" improvements? What is the plan for implementing them?
- Does this affect the business case? If so, how?
- Given your understanding of the problem or gap, do we need to change the charter?

ANALYZE: Causes

Goal:

Identify deep causes and confirm them with data

Output:

A theory that has been tested and confirmed

Critical Checkpoints:

- Potential causes identified
- The root causes or vital few factors verified by data

Relevant Tools:

Checksheets, concentration diagrams, detailed flow-charts, work-flow diagrams, cycle time analysis, frequency plots, hypothesis testing, cause-and-effect diagrams, scatter plots, regression analysis, and designed experiments

Useful Questions:

- How did you identify potential causes? Show me the tool you used and/or the data you collected.
    - If you used a cause-and-effect diagram, walk me through it.

- If you used another tool (such as a scatter plot, regression analysis, frequency plot, hypothesis testing, tree diagram, or designed experiment), tell me what data you collected to construct the plot. What did you conclude?

- If you used process mapping and analysis, walk through the relevant flowcharts.

• Which of the factors turned out to be root causes or to contribute most to the problem?

• How did you verify these root causes or vital few factors? How did you analyze the data? Show me your charts or graphs.

• How do you know you've gotten at root causes and not just symptoms?

• Which factors will you investigate further? How did you choose them? What graphs or statistics support your choice?

• Does identification of root causes affect the make-up of the team?

• Does this affect the business case? If so, how?

• Have you found any "quick hit" improvements?

IMPROVE: Solutions

Goal:

Develop, test, and implement solutions that address deep causes

Output:

Planned, tested actions that should eliminate or reduce the impact of the identified root causes

Critical Checkpoints:

- Several possible solutions generated
- One or more solutions chosen and tested on a small scale
- Small-scale tests show that one or more solutions address the problem
- Plans for full-scale implementation developed and carried out
- Pilot plans checked and learnings applied to implementation plans

Relevant Tools:

Checksheets, work-flow diagrams, flowcharts, prioritization matrix, cost-benefit analysis, FMEA, EMEA, designed experiments, Gantt chart and other planning tools, stakeholder analysis and other change management tools

Useful Questions:

- How did you generate your potential solutions?
- What criteria did you use to evaluate the potential solutions? How do the criteria relate to the key performance measures?
- Show me your prioritization matrix.
- What potential problems, errors, or failure modes did you identify? How were they addressed?
- Which solutions did you pilot test? How did you test them? If you tested several changes, did you use a designed experiment?
- Show me the data you collected during the pilot tests. What was the impact on the root causes and key performance indicators or measures?
- Show me your cost-benefit analysis.
- Show me the plan for full implementation.
- If appropriate, show me the revised flowcharts that describe the new process.
- What steps can be taken to manage the cultural impact of the full-scale implementation? Who will be affected by the changes and how? What is being done to facilitate this change?
- Describe the business case for full-scale implementation of the chosen solution(s). How will this affect customers?

IMPROVE: Results

Goal:

Use data to evaluate the solutions and the implementation plans

Output:

- Before-and-after data analysis that shows how much of original gap was closed
- A comparison of the plan to implementation results

Critical Checkpoints:

- Results checked against the performance indicators, the customer measures identified in DEFINE: Project, and/or the baseline measures quantified in MEASURE: Current Situation
- Actual implementation checked against the plan

Relevant Tools:

Pareto charts, time plots, control charts, frequency plots, hypothesis testing, and process sigma calculation

Useful Questions:

- What are the results of the full-scale implementation?
- Show me your before-and-after data. How much of the original gap was closed? How much remains?
- What is the new process sigma?
- Have the definitions of defect, unit, and opportunity changed?
- What did you do to address the technical and cultural impacts of this change?
- Was the business case realized?
- Did you identify unexpected side effects?
- What unexpected problems did you encounter? Where did you deviate from the plan? What happened?

CONTROL: Standardization

Goal:

Maintain the gains by consistently implementing the new work methods or processes

Output:

- Documentation of the new method
- Training in the new method
- A system for monitoring its consistent use and checking the results

Critical Checkpoints:

- Work methods or processes needed to hold the gains documented and used
- A monitoring plan put in place to ensure continued use of the standard method or process
- Organizational systems such as training developed to support the standardization

Relevant Tools:

Checksheets, work-flow diagrams, flowcharts, time plots, control charts, and process management charts

Useful Questions:

- What is the new standard method or process? How was it developed?
- How is the new method documented? Where is the documentation kept? How will employees access it?
- Who owns the process?
  - Who will maintain and update documentation?
  - Who will check to make sure that the standard methods or processes are used? How often?
- Show me your plan for process management. What will be measured? How often? By whom? How will the data be displayed? Where will control charts be used? What action will be taken if the measurements are unsatisfactory?
- How will you transfer responsibility for ongoing monitoring to the process owner?
- What organizational systems need to change to support standardization?

CONTROL: Future Plans

Goal:

Anticipate future improvements and preserve the lessons from this effort

Output:

Complete documentation and communication of results, learnings, and recommendations

Critical Checkpoints:

- Project documentation completed
- Plan for communicating results and learnings developed
- Remaining gaps documented

Relevant Tools:

Pareto charts, time plots, and control charts

Useful Questions:

- Show me your project documentation.
- What did you learn from this project about making improvements, planning, working as a team, etc.? To whom should these learnings be communicated? How?
- How will the project be brought to a close? How will you celebrate your efforts?

- What other areas of the organization can benefit from your method? How might we get them to adopt the new methods or processes?

- What additional gaps did you identify? How did you document them?

- What recommendations do you have for addressing these gaps?

Design Project Review

Define Project

Goal:

Develop a clear definition of the project

Output:

- Charter
- Project plan
- Organizational change plan
- Review plan

Critical Checkpoints:

- Charter documented
- Project plan documented (detailed plans for next step; high level plans for rest of project)
- Organizational change and communication plans documented
- Review schedule documented

Relevant Tools:

- Market analysis tools (market forecasting tools; customer value analysis; technology forecasting and visioning; competitor analysis)
- Process analysis tools (trend charts; Pareto charts; process management charts)
- Project planning tools and software (work breakdown structure; PERT charts; GANTT charts)
- Project scoping tools (In-Scope/Out-of-Scope tool)

Useful Questions:

- What are the strategic drivers for the project?
- What is the problem we are trying to address?
- Why is improvement or PDCA not adequate?
- What is the scope of the project?
- What is the timeline for completion?
- What team resources are needed?
- What are the major risks associated with the project? How will risks be addressed?
- How can we make sure the organization embraces and supports the changes resulting from the design?

Establish Requirements

Goals:

- Collect Voice of the Customer data
- Translate VOC into design requirements (KQCs)
- Identify the most important KQCs

Output:

Prioritized KQCs

Critical Checkpoints:

- Customer segmentation strategy identified
- Top 10-15 customer needs documented
- Top 8-10 KQCs and targets documented
- Benchmark information summarized
- Platform management matrix developed
- KQC achievement matrix documented

Relevant Tools:

- Data collection plan
- Customer segmentation
- Customer research (contextual inquiry; interviews; focus groups; surveys)
- Kano model
- Affinity diagram
- Benchmarking
- QFD (Quality Function Deployment)

Useful Questions:

- Who are the customers of the service?
- Who are the most important customers?
- Do all customers have the same needs?
- How can the customers be segmented?
- How did we collect data on customers' needs?
- How did we understand customers' most important needs?
- What are the critical design requirements to meet the customers' needs?
- What performance targets should the design meet to satisfy customers?
- What are the risks associated with not meeting all performance requirements immediately?
- Is a phased approach necessary to meet all key KQCs?

Select Concept

Goal:

To evaluate and select the concept that best meets the KQCs within budget and resource constraints

Output:

A selected concept for further analysis and design

Critical Checkpoints:

- List of key functions selected
- List of top concepts selected
- Pugh Matrix completed
- Concept review outputs documented
- Risk analysis updated

Relevant Tools:

- QFD
- Creativity Tools
- Benchmarking
- Pugh Matrix

Useful Questions:

- What are the most important functions or processes that must be designed to meet the design requirements?
- What are the key inputs and outputs of each process?
- Which functions or processes require innovative new designs to maintain a competitive advantage?
- What are the different solutions available for designing each function or process?
- What criteria did we use to evaluate these design alternatives?
- How do we collect information on these criteria that will help us effectively evaluate these designs?
- How does the selected concept affect the features included in the base design and in platform extensions?

Generate Design

Goals:

- Develop high level and detailed design
- Test design components
- Prepare for pilot and full scale deployment

Output:

- Tested high level design
- Tested detailed design
- Plans for process control and pilot
- Completed design reviews

Critical Checkpoints for High Level Design:

- High level design requirements prioritized and documented
- Paper design of key elements complete
- Results from simulation/prototyping documented
- Cost/benefit analysis results documented
- High risk areas identified and risk mitigation plans developed

Critical Checkpoints for Detailed Design:

- Design fully developed and tested
- FMEA/EMEA/simulation analysis completed

- Solutions designed for vulnerable elements
- Process management system variables identified
- Process management system details documented

Relevant Tools:

- QFD
- Simulation
- Rapid prototyping
- FMEA/EMEA
- Planning tools
- Design reviews

Useful Questions:

- How many intermediate levels of design are necessary before all decisions are made?
- What are the key elements of the design that must be considered?
- How do we prioritize these elements?
- How do we partition the design work into sub-teams?
- How do we ensure that these sub-teams communicate effectively with each other during the design process?
- How do we test the design on paper to get a degree of confidence that it will work before implementation?
- How do we identify weak points in the design that may be susceptible to failure?
- How do we test the design after it is complete?

Implement Design

Goals:

- "Stress-testing" and de-bugging of prototype
- Implementation and team closure

Output:

- Working prototype with documentation
- Plans for full implementation
- Process owners using control plans to measure, monitor, and maintain process capability
- Project closure and completed documentation
- Ownership transitioned to operations

Critical Checkpoints:

- Pilot is conducted and completed
- Pilot results are checked against performance requirements; pilot implementation and process management activities are checked against plans, and revisions are made as necessary
- Implementation plans are documented
- First phase of implementation is complete; results and plans have been checked and changes made as appropriate
- Organizational change plans are revised and documented
- Project is closed

Relevant Tools:

- Planning tools
- Appropriate data analysis tools (control charts; Pareto charts)
- Standardization tools (flowcharts; checklists)
- Process management tools (process management charts)
- Project documentation

Useful Questions:

- How do we ensure the pilot is realistic and produces meaningful results?
- What actions must be taken if the pilot performance is unsatisfactory?
- How do we make sure that the performance of a successful design can be sustained over time?
- How do we reward and celebrate the design team?
- How can we ensure that the learnings of the design team (tools and process) are available to the entire organization?
- How can we make sure that the organization embraces and supports the changes resulting from the design?

Appendix

Table of Contents

The Relationship Between Design and Improvement

The design methodology can be used to redesign existing processes, services, and products when they require breakthrough improvements, or to design new processes, services, and products.

Both improvement and design projects rely on excellent process management to ensure that improvement solutions and new designs are adequately maintained and supported by the organization. The decision tree on the next page can help you decide when to use which methodology.

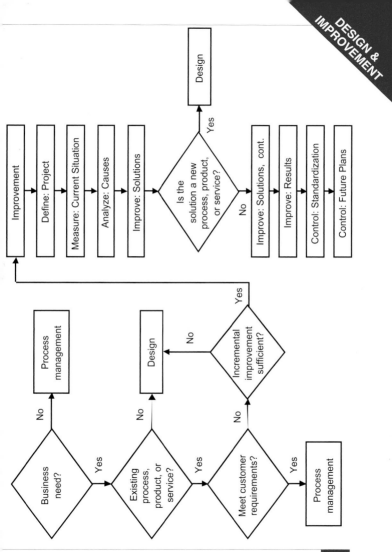

Improvement → Define: Project → Measure: Current Situation → Analyze: Causes → Improve: Solutions → Is the solution a new process, product, or service?

Is the solution a new process, product, or service? — Yes → Design

Is the solution a new process, product, or service? — No → Improve: Solutions, cont. → Improve: Results → Control: Standardization → Control: Future Plans

Incremental improvement sufficient? — Yes → Improvement

Incremental improvement sufficient? — No → Design

Business need? — No → Process management

Business need? — Yes → Existing process, product, or service?

Existing process, product, or service? — No → Design

Existing process, product, or service? — Yes → Meet customer requirements?

Meet customer requirements? — No → Incremental improvement sufficient?

Meet customer requirements? — Yes → Process management

33

Tollgate Reviews

What Are They?

Tollgate reviews are project reviews that the project sponsors and/or the leadership team conduct on a regular schedule. These reviews allow the sponsor and leadership team to monitor the progress of a project and ensure that the team has completed each step with sufficient rigor.

When Are They Done?

Tollgate reviews should occur at the end of each step in the improvement and design methods.

Why Are They Important?

- Establish a common understanding of the efforts to date and monitor progress
- Ensure alignment and reinforce priorities
- Provide guidance and direction for the organization
- Demonstrate support for the project and model behavior
- Provide ongoing coaching and instruction
- Recognize the team's efforts (to foster intrinsic motivation for improvements)
- Gather data from the organization, enabling better planning at your level
- Ensure continuous progress by the team

Improvement Project Review Template

Step	Date Completed	Date Reviewed	Notes from Review	Follow-up Action	
				Who	By When
DEFINE: Project					
MEASURE: Current Situation					
ANALYZE: Causes					
IMPROVE: Solutions					
IMPROVE: Results					
CONTROL: Standardization					
CONTROL: Future Plans					

Design Project Review Template

Step	Date Completed	Date Reviewed	Notes from Review	Follow-up Action	
				Who	By When
Define Project					
Establish Requirements					
Select Concept					
Generate Design					
Impleme**N**t Design					

Tollgate Review Flowchart

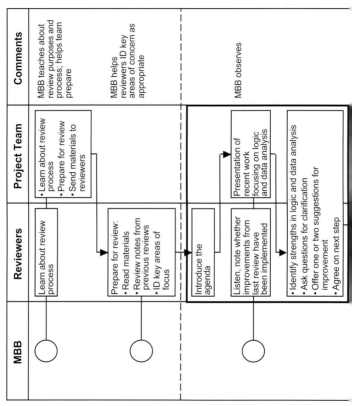

MBB	Reviewers	Project Team	Comments
○	Learn about review process	• Learn about review process • Prepare for review • Send materials to reviewers	MBB teaches about review purposes and process; helps team prepare
○	Prepare for review: • Read materials • Review notes from previous reviews • ID key areas of focus		MBB helps reviewers ID key areas of concern as appropriate
○	Introduce the agenda		MBB observes
	Listen, note whether improvements from last review have been implemented	Presentation of recent work focusing on logic and data analysis	
	• Identify strengths in logic and data analysis • Ask questions for clarification • Offer one or two suggestions for improvement • Agree on next step		

Before Review Meeting

During Review Meeting

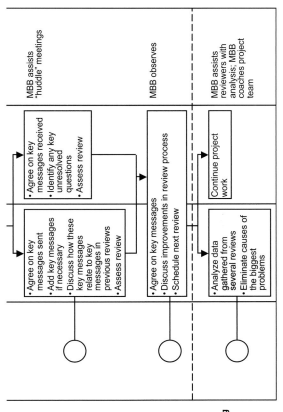

MBB assists "huddle" meetings

MBB observes

MBB assists reviewers with analysis; MBB coaches project team

- Agree on key messages received
- Identify any key unresolved questions
- Assess review

Continue project work

- Agree on key messages sent
- Add key messages if necessary
- Discuss how these key messages relate to key messages in previous reviews
- Assess review

- Agree on key messages
- Discuss improvements in review process
- Schedule next review

- Analyze data gathered from several reviews
- Eliminate causes of the biggest problems

After Review Meeting

37

Project Roles for Improvement and Design

The Sponsor's Role

Before the Project:

- Ensure the project is linked to the larger six sigma effort
- Draft team charter
- Select team leader and coach
- Select team members (with team leader)
- Identify required resources
- Orient team to the project (with team leader)

During the Project:

- Review team progress often
- Provide guidance, direction, and support
- Be an unwavering advocate for customer and data
- When necessary, intervene to remove barriers to success
- Ensure that cross-functional and cross-business linkages work smoothly
- Monitor other initiatives for potential overlap or conflicts
- Ensure continued monitoring of key processes and measures

- Inform leadership team and others of progress and learnings
- Integrate the team's work with the larger six sigma effort
- Help transition responsibility from project team to organization during implementation

After the Project:

- Celebrate the project's conclusion
- Ensure solutions are implemented
- Ensure project results are quantified and documented
- Preserve and apply lessons learned

The Leadership Team's Role

- Establish strategic direction
- Develop an organizational approach to working toward six sigma
- Choose key improvement and/or design projects that are linked to business needs
- For design projects, identify market drivers for the new product or service
- Identify a sponsor for each project
- Identify process owner(s) and ensure their appropriate involvement in the project
- Manage project "pipeline" by:
  - Approving charters
  - Coordinating and integrating projects

- Review progress
- Approve recommended solutions and funding
- Ensure that the organization's management systems can support the design or maintain the improvement gains across the business
- Recognize and communicate team's efforts

Project Leader Role

Because these projects, especially design projects, are often strategic and represent significant investments, the team leader role can be extensive. Project team leaders often:

- Are senior, experienced project managers with multidisciplinary skills
- Have direct responsibility for the success of the project
- Actively champion the concept and the method
- In strategic projects, may have authority over people working on the project

Before the project they:

- Review the charter with the sponsor
- Draft remaining charter elements
- Partner with sponsor to identify team resources

During the project they:

- Serve as liaison to the organization, along with coach, sponsor, and other stakeholders, to ensure relevant information is communicated regarding the project
- Lead the team
- Contribute knowledge and expertise
- Maintain records and project documentation
- Manage the team's progress against schedule and adjust as required to meet deliverables
- Manage team dynamics

After the project they:

- Ensure that documentation is completed and available for others

Team Composition

A critical success factor for teams is to make sure all the key functions and skills are represented in the core team. For example, a team may need members from engineering, operations, information technology, risk management, finance, marketing, sales, and distribution. In addition, a blend of experience, "young blood," and a diversity of perspectives is desirable. It is a good idea to review team membership at the end of each phase. You may need to add or change members for the work in the upcoming phase.

Sigma Look-Up Table

Sigma	DPMO	YIELD	Sigma	DPMO	YIELD
6	3.4	99.99966%	2.9	80,757	91.9%
5.9	5.4	99.99946%	2.8	96,801	90.3%
5.8	8.5	99.99915%	2.7	115,070	88.5%
5.7	13	99.99866%	2.6	135,666	86.4%
5.6	21	99.9979%	2.5	158,655	84.1%
5.5	32	99.9968%	2.4	184,060	81.6%
5.4	48	99.9952%	2.3	211,855	78.8%
5.3	72	99.9928%	2.2	241,964	75.8%
5.2	108	99.9892%	2.1	274,253	72.6%
5.1	159	99.984%	2	308,538	69.1%
5	233	99.977%	1.9	344,578	65.5%
4.9	337	99.966%	1.8	382,089	61.8%
4.8	483	99.952%	1.7	420,740	57.9%
4.7	687	99.931%	1.6	460,172	54.0%
4.6	968	99.90%	1.5	500,000	50.0%
4.5	1,350	99.87%	1.4	539,828	46.0%
4.4	1,866	99.81%	1.3	579,260	42.1%
4.3	2,555	99.74%	1.2	617,911	38.2%
4.2	3,467	99.65%	1.1	655,422	34.5%
4.1	4,661	99.53%	1	691,462	30.9%
4	6,210	99.38%	0.9	725,747	27.4%
3.9	8,198	99.18%	0.8	758,036	24.2%
3.8	10,724	98.9%	0.7	788,145	21.2%
3.7	13,903	98.6%	0.6	815,940	18.4%
3.6	17,864	98.2%	0.5	841,345	15.9%
3.5	22,750	97.7%	0.4	864,334	13.6%
3.4	28,716	97.1%	0.3	884,930	11.5%
3.3	35,930	96.4%	0.2	903,199	9.7%
3.2	44,565	95.5%	0.1	919,243	8.1%
3.1	54,799	94.5%			
3	66,807	93.3%			

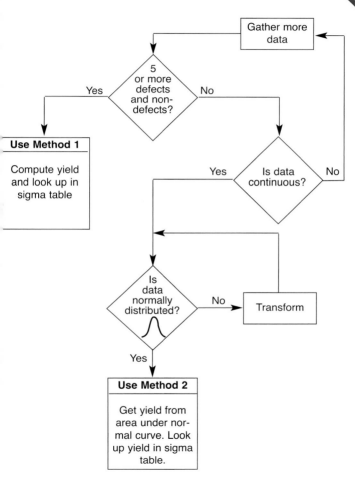

Sigma Calculation Form: Method

1. Determine number of defect opportunities per unit **O =**	
2. Determine number of units processed **N =**	
3. Determine total number of defects made (include defects made and later fixed) **D =**	
4. Calculate Defects Per Opportunity $\mathbf{DPO} = \dfrac{D}{N \times O} =$	
5. Calculate Yield **Yield** = (1-DPO) x 100 =	
6. Look up Sigma in the Process Sigma Table **Process Sigma =**	

Example: Sigma Method 1

1. Determine number of defect opportunities per unit	**O =**	5
2. Determine number of units processed	**N =**	100
3. Determine total number of defects made (include defects made and later fixed)	**D =**	7
4. Calculate Defects Per Opportunity	$\mathbf{DPO} = \dfrac{D}{N \times O} =$	.014
5. Calculate Yield	**Yield** $= (1 - DPO) \times 100 =$	98.6
6. Look up Sigma in the Process Sigma Table	**Process Sigma =**	3.7

Sigma Calculation Form: Method 2

1. Enter Average, Standard Deviation, and Spec Limits

$\overline{X}$ = _____   s = _____   USL = _____   LSL = _____

2. Label a Normal Curve

- Average
- Standard deviation
- USL (and shade to LEFT for Area 1)
- LSL (and shade to LEFT for Area 2)

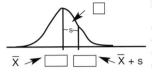

$\overline{X}$ ➤ ☐ ☐ ◄ $\overline{X}$ + s

3. Determine Area below USL (Area 1)

Find Z_1 $\dfrac{\text{USL} - \overline{X}}{s}$ $\dfrac{(\quad) - (\quad)}{(\quad)}$ ☐

Look up Z_1 NormDist (Z_1) = Value from Normal Table =   ☐
in Normal Table

4. Determine Area below LSL, if any (Area 2)

Find Z_2 $Z_2 = \dfrac{\text{LSL} - \overline{X}}{s}$ = $\dfrac{(\quad) - (\quad)}{(\quad)}$ =   ☐

Look up Z_2 NormDist (Z_2) = Value from Normal Table =   ☐
in Normal Table

5. Calculate Yield

Yield = Area 1 - Area 2 = _____ - _____ =   ☐

Yield $_{(\text{percentage})}$ = Yield x 100% =   ☐

6. Look up Yield in Process Sigma Table

Proces Sigma = Look up from Sigma Table =   ☐

Example: Sigma Calculation Method 2

1. Enter Average, Standard Deviation, and Spec Limits

$\overline{X} =$ __17__ $s =$ __3__   USL = __25__   LSL = __N/A__

2. Label a Normal Curve

- Average
- Standard deviation
- USL (and shade to LEFT for Area 1)
- LSL (and shade to LEFT for Area 2)

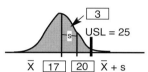

$\boxed{3}$
USL = 25

$\overline{X}$ $\boxed{17}$ $\boxed{20}$ $\overline{X} + s$

3. Determine Area below USL (Area 1)

Find Z_1 $Z_1 = \dfrac{USL - \overline{X}}{s} = \dfrac{(\ 25\ ) - (\ 17\ )}{(\ 3\ )} =$ $\boxed{2.67}$

Look up Z_1 in Normal Table   NormDist (Z_1) = Value from Normal Table = $\boxed{.996533}$

4. Determine Area below LSL, if any (Area 2)

Find Z_2 $Z_2 = \dfrac{LSL - \overline{X}}{s} = \dfrac{(\quad) - (\quad)}{(\quad)} =$ $\boxed{N/A}$

Look up Z_2 in Normal Table   NormDist (Z_2) = Value from Normal Table = $\boxed{}$

5. Calculate Yield

Yield = Area 1 - Area 2 = .996533 - __0__ = $\boxed{.996533}$

Yield (percentage) = Yield x 100% = $\boxed{99.65\%}$

6. Look up Yield in Process Sigma Table

Proces Sigma = Look up from Sigma Table = $\boxed{4.2}$

Glossary

Affinity diagram: A tool that helps organize language data into related groupings.

Benchmarking: A method for identifying world class products, processes, or services and acquiring a deep understanding of how and why they work.

Cause-and-effect diagram: A tool used to identify and organize possible causes of a problem in a structured format. It is sometimes called a fishbone diagram because it looks like the skeleton of a fish.

Charter: A written document that describes the work of the team.

Checklist: A list of action items, steps, or elements needed for a task. Each item is checked off as it is completed.

Checksheet: A form used to collect data by making tally marks to indicate the number of times something occurs. Checksheets help standardize the data that is collected and the data collection process.

Concentration diagram: A type of checksheet in which you write on a picture of the object about which you are collecting data.

Concept review: A design review conducted after one or two key design concepts have been identified and their feasibility has been determined.

Contextual inquiry: A data gathering method used to collect latent customer needs.

Control chart: A time plot that includes a centerline and upper and lower control limits. These limits allow you to quickly detect specific changes in a process.

Cost-benefit analysis: Evaluation of the financial impact of proposed solutions or actions.

Cycle time analysis: The study of how much time it takes for work to flow through a process. You can identify bottlenecks and inefficiencies by looking at the work time and the wait time in each process step.

Data: Clearly defined measurements of characteristics. They are most useful when collected to monitor or improve a process.

Defect: Any measurable event that does not meet a customer specification.

Defect opportunity: A measurable chance for a defect to occur.

Defective: A unit with one or more defects.

Delighter needs: Product or service characteristics which customers do not mention because they are not dissatisfied with their absence. Often, customers have not thought these characteristics were possible.

Designed experiments: The systematic and simultaneous testing of multiple process inputs or variables to study their effect on the output.

Detailed design review: A design review (also called a pre-pilot design review) conducted when the detailed design is complete and the product or service is ready to be piloted.

DPMO: The number of defects per million opportunities.

EMEA: Error modes and effects analysis is used to identify potential errors related to human performance.

Flowchart: A picture of the sequence of steps in a process in which different steps are represented by boxes or other symbols. Can be adapted to show hand-offs or to highlight value-added steps.

FMEA: Failure modes and effects analysis is used to identify potential equipment and machinery failures.

Frequency plot: A graphic tool that shows the shape or distribution of the data by showing how often different values occur. This makes it easier to see what is happening with the data and to identify some types of process problems.

Gantt chart: A chart of a project schedule that shows the order and duration of tasks.

Gage R&R: An investigation of the repeatability and reproducability of the measurement system in order to determine the sources and amount of measurement variation.

High level design review: A design review conducted after a concept has been designed to some level of detail and tested, and before detailed design begins.

Hypothesis testing: A statistical procedure to determine if subgroups or strata give results that differ significantly.

Kano model: A model developed by Noriaki Kano which defines 3 categories of customer needs: must-be needs, satisfiers, and delighters.

KQC: Key Quality Characteristic of a product or service which contains the following elements: the characteristic, a measure for the performance of the characteristic, a target value, and specification limits for the measure. KQCs are also called design requirements.

KQC achievement matrix: Also called a KQC risk matrix, this tool summarizes the thinking about risks associated with not meeting target performance requirements.

Latent needs: Customer needs that may not be verbalized and have to be extracted in a VOC study.

Must-be needs: Characteristics which customers generally take for granted.

Operational definition: A precise description that tells how to get a value for the characteristic you are trying to measure. Often a cut-off for what is to be considered defective is included.

Pareto chart: A graphic tool that helps break a big problem down into its parts and identify which parts are most important.

PDCA: The plan-do-check-act cycle is an approach to improvement that emphasizes planning a set of actions and how to collect data on their effectiveness, implementing the actions, checking the data, and acting on the data.

Pilot test: A small-scale test of a proposed solution.